Presented to:

_____

From:

_____

Date:

_____

THE ILLUSTRATED BAPTIST CATECHISM

Illustrated by
Paul Cox

Table of Contents

And these words, which I command thee this day, shall be in thine heart:

And thou shalt teach them diligently unto thy children, and shalt talk of them when thou sittest in thine house, and when thou walkest by the way, and when thou liest down, and when thou risest up.

And thou shalt bind them for a sign upon thine hand, and they shall be as frontlets between thine eyes.

Deuteronomy 6:6–8

To my children:
May this be a tool for growth
in the knowledge of our Lord
and Savior, Jesus Christ.

Introduction

The Baptist Catechism, or Keach's Catechism, is a Bible based teaching tool composed of a series of questions and answers with the purpose of teaching the basic doctrines of the Christian faith. It is based on the 1689 London Baptist Confession of Faith and was first published in 1693.

Section I
God's Word

Question #1

Who is the first and chiefest being?

Answer

God is the first and chiefest being.

Isa 44:6; 48:12; Psa 97:9

Ought everyone
to believe there
is a God?

Answer

Everyone ought to believe
there is a God; and it is
their great sin and folly
who do not.

Heb 11:6; Psa 14:1

Question #3

How may we know there is a God?

Answer

The light of nature in man and the works of God plainly declare there is a God; but His Word and Spirit only do it fully and effectually for the salvation of sinners.

Rom 1:19-20; Psa 19:1-3; Act 17:24; 1Co 2:10; 2Ti 3:15-16

Question #4

What is the Word of God?

Answer

The holy Scriptures of the Old and New Testament are the Word of God, and the only certain rule of faith and obedience.

2Ti 3:16; Eph 2:20

Question #5

May all men make use of the holy Scriptures?

Answer

All men are not only permitted, but commanded and exhorted to read, hear, and understand the holy Scriptures.

Joh 5:38; 17:17-18; Rev 1:3; Act 8:30

Question #6

What things are chiefly contained in the holy Scriptures?

Answer

The holy Scriptures chiefly contain what man ought to believe concerning God, and what duty God requireth of man.

2Ti 1:13; 3:15-16

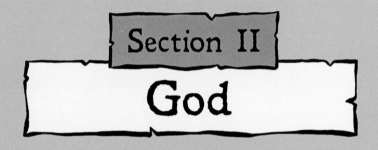

Section II

God

Question #7

What is God?

Answer

God is a Spirit, infinite, eternal; and unchangeable in His being, wisdom, power, holiness, justice, goodness, and truth.

Joh 4:24; Job 11:7-9; Psa 110:2; Jam 1:17;
Exo 3:14; Psa 147:5; Rev 4:8; Rev 15:4; Exo 34:6

Question #8

Are there
more gods
than one?

Answer

There is but one only:
the living and true God.

Deu 6:4; Jer 10:10

Question #9

How many persons are there in the Godhead?

Answer

There are three persons in the Godhead: the Father, the Son, and the Holy Spirit; and these three are one God, the same in essence, equal in power and glory.

1Jo 5:7; Mat 28:19

Question #10

What are the decrees of God?

Answer

The decrees of God are His eternal purpose according to the counsel of His will, whereby, for His own glory, He hath foreordained whatsoever comes to pass.

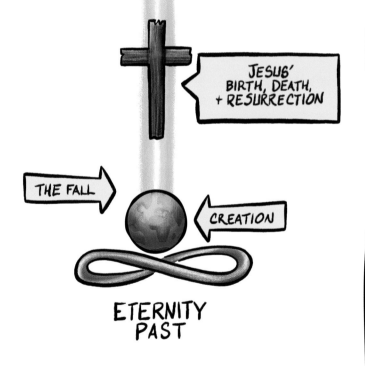

Eph 1:4, 11; Rom 9:22-23; Isa 46:10; Lam 3:37

Question #11

How doth God execute his decrees?

Answer

God executeth His decrees in the works of creation and providence.

Gen 1:1; Rev 4:11; Mat 6:26; Act 14:17

Question #12

What is the work of creation?

Answer

The work of creation is God's making all things of nothing, by the word of his power, in the space of six days, and all very good.

Gen 1; Heb 11:3

Question #13

How did God create man?

Answer

God created man, male and female, after His own image, in knowledge, righteousness, and holiness, with dominion over the creatures.

Gen 1:26-28; Col 3:10, Eph 4:24

Question #14

What are God's works of providence?

Answer

God's works of providence are His most holy, wise, and powerful preserving and governing all His creatures, and all their actions.

Psa 145:17; Isa 28:29, Psa 104:24; Heb 1:3; Psa 103:19; Mat 10:29-31

Question #15

What special act of providence did God exercise towards man in the estate wherein he was created?

Answer

When God had created man, He entered into a covenant of life with him upon condition of perfect obedience: forbidding him to eat of the tree of the knowledge of good and evil, upon pain of death.

Gal 3:12; Gen 2:17

Section III
Sin

Question #16

Did our first parents continue in the estate wherein they were created?

Answer

Our first parents, being left to the freedom of their own will, fell from the estate wherein they were created by sinning against God.

Gen 3:6-8, 13; Ecc 7:29

Question #17

What is sin?

Answer

Sin is any want of conformity unto, or transgression of, the law of God.

1Jo 3:4

Question #18

What was the sin whereby our first parents fell from the estate wherein they were created?

Answer

The sin whereby our first parents fell from the estate wherein they were created, was their eating the forbidden fruit.

Gen 3:6, 12, 16-17

Question #19

Did all mankind fall in Adam's first transgression?

Answer

The covenant being made with Adam, not only for himself but for his posterity, all mankind descending from him by ordinary generation sinned in him, and fell with him in his first transgression.

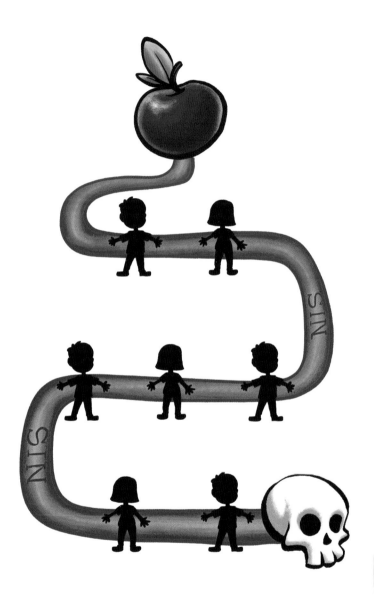

Gen 2:16-17; Rom 5:12; 1Co 15:21-22

Question #20

Into what estate did the **Fall** bring mankind?

Answer

The **Fall** brought mankind into an estate of sin and misery.

Rom 5:12

Question #21

Wherein consists the sinfulness of that estate whereinto man fell?

Answer

The sinfulness of that estate whereinto man fell, consists in the guilt of Adam's first sin, the want of original righteousness, and the corruption of his whole nature, which is commonly called original sin, together with all actual transgressions which proceed from it.

Gen 2:16-17; Rom 5:12; Eph 2:1-3; Jam 1:14-15; Mat 15:19; 1Co 15:21-22

Question #22

What is the misery of that estate whereinto man fell?

Answer

All mankind by their fall lost communion with God, are under His wrath and curse, and so made liable to all miseries in this life, to death itself, and to the pains of hell forever.

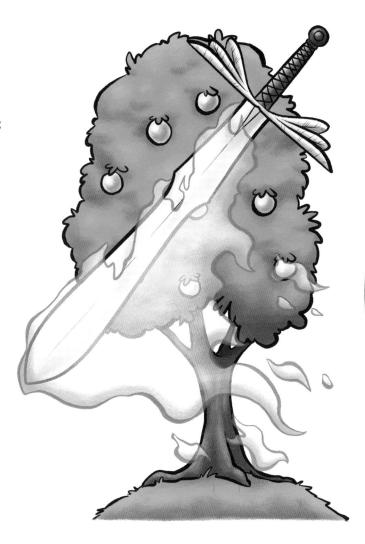

Gen 3:8, 10, 24; Eph 2:2-3; Gal 3:10; Lam 3:39; Rom 6:23; Mat 25:41, 46

Section IV
Jesus Christ

Did God leave all mankind to perish in the estate of sin and misery?

Answer

God—having out of His mere good pleasure, from all eternity, elected some to everlasting life—did enter into a Covenant of Grace, to deliver them out of the estate of sin and misery, and to bring them into an estate of salvation by a Redeemer.

Eph 1:4-5; Rom 3:20-22; Gal 3:21-22

Who is the
Redeemer of
God's elect?

Answer

The only Redeemer of God's
elect is the Lord Jesus Christ;
Who, being the eternal Son of
God, became man, and so was
and continueth to be God and
man in two distinct natures,
and one person forever.

1Ti 2:5, 6; Joh 1:14; Gal 4:4; Rom 9:5;
Luk 1:35; Col 2:9; Heb 7:24, 25

Question #25

How did Christ, being the Son of God, become man?

Answer

Christ, the Son of God, became man by taking to Himself a true body and a reasonable soul; being conceived by the power of the Holy Spirit in the womb of the Virgin Mary, and born of her, yet without sin.

Heb 2:14, 17; 10:5; Mat 26:38;
Luk 1:27, 31, 34-35, 42; Gal 4:4; Heb 4:15; 7:26

Question #26

What offices doth Christ execute as our Redeemer?

Answer

Christ as our Redeemer executeth the offices of a prophet, of a priest, and of king, both in His estate of humiliation and exaltation.

Act 3:22; Heb 12:25; 2Co 13:3; Heb 5:5-7; 7:25; Psa 2:6; Isa 9:6-7; Mat 21:5; Psa 2:8-11

Question #27

How doth Christ execute the office of a prophet?

Answer

Christ executeth the office of prophet in revealing to us, by His Word and Spirit, the will of God for our salvation.

Joh 1:18; 1Pe 1:10-12; Joh 15:15; 20:31

Question #28

How doth Christ execute the office of a priest?

Answer

Christ executeth the office of priest in His once offering up Himself a sacrifice to satisfy divine justice and reconcile us to God, and in making continual intercession for us.

Heb 9:14, 28; Heb 2:17; Heb 7:24-25

Question #29

How doth Christ execute the office of king?

Answer

Christ executeth the office of a king, in subduing us to Himself, in ruling and defending us, and in restraining and conquering all His and our enemies.

Act 15:14-16; Isa 33:22; Isa 32:1-2; 1Co 15:25; Psa 110

Question #30

Wherein did Christ's humiliation consist?

Answer

Christ's humiliation consisted in His being born, and that in a low condition, made under the Law; undergoing the miseries of this life, the wrath of God, and the cursed death of the cross; in being buried, and continuing under the power of death for a time.

Luk 2:7; Gal 4:4; Heb 12:2-3; Isa 53:2-3; Luk 22:44; Mat 27:46; Phi 2:8; 1Co 15:3-4; Act 2:24-27, 31; Mat 12:40

Question #31

Wherein consisteth Christ's exaltation?

Answer

Christ's exaltation consisteth in His rising again from the dead on the third day, in ascending up into heaven, in sitting at the right hand of God the Father, and in coming to judge the world at the Last Day.

REMINDERS:
* Judge World — Last Day
* Uphold all things

1Co 15:4; Mar 16:19; Eph 1:20; Act 1:11; 17:31

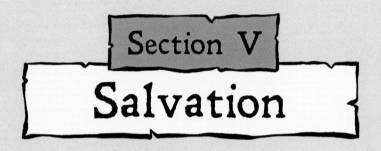

Section V

Salvation

Question #32

How are we made partakers of the redemption purchased by Christ?

Answer

We are made partakers of the redemption purchased by Christ, by the effectual application of it to us by His Holy Spirit.

Joh 1:11-12; Ti 3:5-6

Question #33

How doth the Spirit apply to us the redemption purchased by Christ?

Answer

The Spirit applieth to us the redemption purchased by Christ, by working faith in us, and thereby uniting us to Christ in our effectual calling.

Eph 1:13-14; Joh 6:37, 39; Eph 2:8; Eph 3:17; 1Co 1:9

Question #34

What is effectual calling?

Answer

Effectual calling is the work of God's Spirit whereby—convincing us of our sin and misery, enlightening our minds in the knowledge of Christ, and renewing our wills—He doth persuade and enable us to embrace Jesus Christ freely offered to us in the gospel.

2Ti 1:9; 2Th 2:13-14; Act 2:37; Act 26:18; Eze 36:26-27; Joh 6:44-45; Phi 2:13

Question #35

What benefits do they that are effectually called partake of in this life?

Answer

They that are effectually called do in this life partake of justification, adoption, sanctification, and the several benefits which in this life do either accompany or flow from them.

Rom 8:30; Eph 1:5; 1Co 1:30

What is justification?

Answer

Justification is an act of God's free grace wherein He pardoneth all our sins and accepteth us as righteous in His sight, only for the righteousness of Christ imputed to us and received by faith alone.

Rom 3:24-25; 4:6-8; 2Co 5:19, 21;
Rom 5:17-19; Gal 2:16; Phi 3:9

Question #37

What is adoption?

Answer

Adoption is an act of God's free grace, whereby we are received into the number and have a right to all the privileges of the sons of God.

1Jo 3:1; Joh 1:12; Rom 8:14-17

Question #38

What is sanctification?

Answer

Sanctification is the work of God's free grace whereby we are renewed in the whole man after the image of God, and are enabled more and more to die unto sin and live unto righteousness.

2Th 2:13; Eph 4:23-24; Rom 6:4, 6; Rom 8:1

Question #39

What are the benefits which in this life do accompany or flow from justification, adoption, and sanctification?

Answer

The benefits which in this life do accompany or flow from justification, adoption, and sanctification are assurance of God's love, peace of conscience, joy in the Holy Spirit, increase of grace, and perseverance therein to the end.

Rom 5:1-2, 5, 17; Pro 4:18; 1Jo 5:13; 1Pe 1:5

Question #40

What benefits do believers receive from Christ at their death?

RESTING IN THE ARMS OF CHRIST

Answer

The souls of believers are at their death made perfect in holiness, and do immediately pass into glory; and their bodies being still united to Christ, do rest in their graves till the resurrection.

Heb 12:23; 2Co 5:1, 6, 8; Phi 1:23;
Luk 23:43; 1Th 4:14; Isa 57:2; Job 19:26-27

Question #41

What benefits do believers receive from Christ at the resurrection?

Answer

At the resurrection, believers, being raised up in glory, shall be openly acknowledged and acquitted in the Day of Judgment, and made perfectly blessed both in soul and body, in the full enjoyment of God to all eternity.

1Co 15:43; Mat 25:23; Mat 10:32; 1Jo 3:2; 1Co 13:12; 1Th 4:17-18

Section VI
Judgment

Question #42

But what shall be done to the wicked at their death?

Answer

The souls of the wicked shall, at their death, be cast into the torments of hell, and their bodies lie in their graves till the resurrection and judgment of the great day.

Luk 16:23-24; Act 2:24; Jud 1:5, 7; 1Pe 3:19; Psa 49:14

Question #43

What shall be done to the wicked at the Day of Judgment?

Answer

At the Day of Judgment, the bodies of the wicked, being raised out of their graves, shall be sentenced, together with their souls, to unspeakable torments with the devil and his angels forever.

Joh 5:28-29; Mat 25:41, 46; 2Th 1:8-9

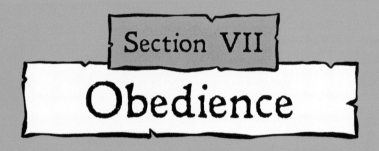

Section VII

Obedience

Question #44

What is the duty which God requireth of man?

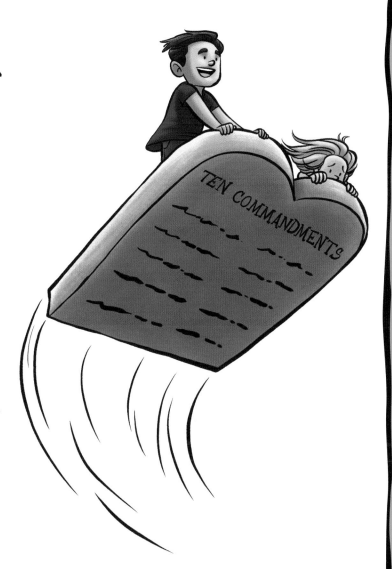

Answer

The duty which God requireth of man is obedience to His revealed will.

Mic 6:8; 1Sa 15:22

Question #45

What did God at first reveal to man for the rule of his obedience?

Answer

The rule which God at first revealed to man for his obedience, was the moral law.

Rom 2:14-15; 10:5

Question #46

Where is the moral law summarily comprehended?

Answer

The moral law is summarily comprehended in the Ten Commandments.

Deu 10:4; Mat 19:17

Question #47

What is
the sum of the
Ten Commandments?

Answer

The sum of the Ten Commandments is to love the Lord our God with all our heart, with all our soul, with all our strength, and with all our mind; and our neighbour as ourselves.

Mat 22:37-40

Question #48

What is the preface to the Ten Commandments?

Answer

The preface to the Ten Commandments is in these words: "I am the Lord thy God, which have brought thee out of the land of Egypt, out of the house of bondage."

Exo 20:2

Question #49

What doth the preface to the Ten Commandments teach us?

Answer

The preface to the Ten Commandments teacheth us that, because God is the Lord, and our God and redeemer, therefore we are bound to keep all His commandments.

Luk 1:74-75; 1Pe 1:15-19

Which is the first commandment?

Answer

The first commandment is, "Thou shalt have no other gods before me."

I

Thou shalt have no other gods before me.

Exo 20:3

Question #51

What is required in the first commandment?

Answer

The first commandment requireth us to know and acknowledge God to be the only true God and our God, and to worship and glorify Him accordingly.

1Ch 28:9; Deu 26:17; Mat 4:10; Psa 29:2

Question #52

What is forbidden in the first commandment?

Answer

The first commandment forbiddeth the denying, or not worshipping and glorifying, the true God as God and our God, and the giving of that worship and glory to any other, which is due unto Him alone.

Psa 14:1; Rom 1:21; Psa 81:10-11; Rom 1:25-26

Question #53

What are we especially taught by these words "before me" in the first commandment?

Answer

These words "before me" in the first commandment teach us that God, Who seeth all things, taketh notice of and is much displeased with the sin of having any other god.

Exo 8:5-32

Question #54

Which is the second commandment?

II

Thou shalt not make unto thee any graven image. Thou shalt not bow down thyself to them, nor serve them.

Answer

The second commandment is, "Thou shalt not make unto thee any graven image, or any likeness of any thing that is in heaven above, or that is in the earth beneath, or that is in the water under the earth: Thou shalt not bow down thyself to them, nor serve them: for I the LORD thy God am a jealous God, visiting the iniquity of the fathers upon the children unto the third and fourth generation of them that hate me; and shewing mercy unto thousands of them that love me, and keep my commandments."

Exo 20:4-6

Question #55

What is required in the second commandment?

Answer

The second commandment requireth the receiving, observing, and keeping pure and entire all such religious worship and ordinances as God hath appointed in His Word.

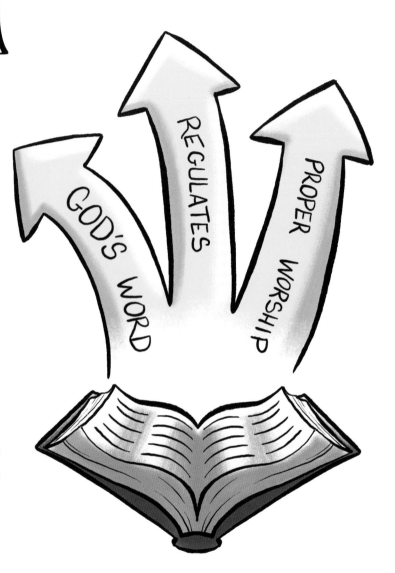

Deu 32:46; Mat 23:20; Act 2:42

Question #56

What is forbidden in the second commandment?

Answer

The second commandment forbiddeth the worshipping of God by images, or any other way not appointed in His Word.

Deu 4:15-19; Exo 32:5, 8; Deu 7:31-32

Question #57

What are the reasons annexed to the second commandment?

Answer

The reasons annexed to the second commandment are God's sovereignty over us, His propriety in us, and the zeal He hath to His own worship.

Psa 45:2-3, 6; Psa 45:11; Exo 34:13-14

Which is
the third
commandment?

Answer

The third commandment is,
"Thou shalt not take the
name of the Lord thy God in
vain; for the Lord will not
hold him guiltless that taketh
His name in vain."

Exo 20:7

75

Question #59

What is required in the third commandment?

Answer

The third commandment requireth the holy and reverent use of God's names, titles, attributes, ordinances, Word, and works.

HOLINESS
SOVEREIGNT
OMNISCIENT
FATHER
ADONAI
OMEGA

Mat 6:9; Deu 28:58; Psa 68:4; Rev 15:3-4;
Mal 1:11, 14; Psa 136: 1-2; Job 36:24

Question #60

What is forbidden in the third commandment?

Answer

The third commandment forbiddeth all profaning and abusing of anything whereby God makes Himself known.

Mal 1:6-7, 12; 2:2; 3:14

Question #61

What is the reason annexed to the third commandment?

Answer

The reason annexed to the third commandment is that, however the breakers of this commandment may escape punishment from men, yet the Lord our God will not suffer them to escape His righteous judgment.

1Sa 2:12, 17, 22, 29; 3:13; Deu 28:58-59

What is
the fourth
commandment?

IV

Remember the
Sabbath day, to
keep it holy.

Answer

The fourth commandment is, "Remember the Sabbath day, to keep it
holy. Six days shalt thou labor, and
do all thy work; but the seventh day
is the Sabbath of the LORD thy
God: in it thou shalt not do any
work, thou, nor thy son, nor thy
daughter, thy manservant, nor thy
maidservant, nor thy cattle, nor thy
stranger that is within thy gates: for
in six days the LORD made heaven
and earth, the sea, and all that in
them is, and rested the seventh day:
wherefore the LORD blessed the
Sabbath day, and hallowed it."

Exo 20:8-11

Question #63

What is required in the fourth commandment?

Answer

The fourth commandment requireth the keeping holy to God such set times as He hath appointed in His Word, expressly, one whole day in seven to be a holy Sabbath to Himself.

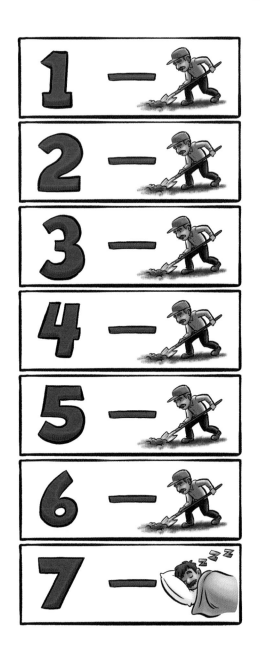

Exo 20:8-11; Deu 5:12-14

Question #64

Which day of the seven hath God appointed to be the weekly Sabbath?

Answer

Before the resurrection of Christ, God appointed the seventh day of the week to be the weekly Sabbath; and the first day of the week ever since, to continue to the end of the world, which is the Christian Sabbath.

Exo 20:8-11; Deu 5:12-14; Psa 118:24; Mat 28:1; Mar 2:27-28; Joh 20:19-20, 26; Rev 1:10; Mar 16:2; Luk 24:1, 30-36; Joh 20:1; Act 1:3; 2:1-2; 20:7; 1Co 16:1-2

Question #65

How is the Sabbath to be sanctified?

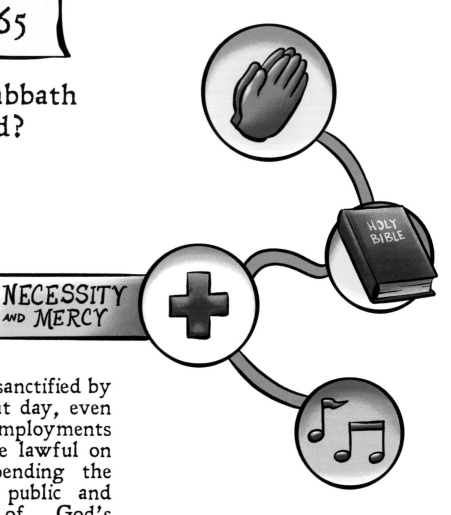

Answer

NECESSITY AND MERCY

The Sabbath is to be sanctified by a holy resting all that day, even from such worldly employments and recreations as are lawful on other days; and spending the whole time in the public and private exercises of God's worship, except so much as is to be taken up in the works of necessity and mercy.

Exo 20:8, 10; Exo 16:25-28; Neh 13:15-22; Luk 4:16;
Act 20:7; Psa 92 title; Isa 66:23; Mat 12:1-13

Question #66

What is forbidden in the fourth commandment?

Answer

The fourth commandment forbideth the omission or careless performance of the duties required, and the profaning the day by idleness, or doing that which is in itself sinful, or by unnecessary thoughts, words, or works about worldly employments or recreations.

Eze 22:26; Amo 8:5; Mal 1:13; Act 20:7, 9; Eze 23:38; Jer 17:24-27; Isa 58:13

Question #67

What are
the reasons
annexed to the
fourth commandment?

Answer

The reasons annexed to the fourth
commandment are God's allowing
us six days of the week for our own
lawful employments, His challeng-
ing a special propriety in a seventh,
His own example, and His blessing
the Sabbath day.

Exo 20:9, 11

Question #68

Which is
the fifth
commandment?

Answer

The fifth commandment is,
"Honor thy father and thy
mother; that thy days may be
long upon the land which the
Lord thy God giveth thee."

Exo 20:12

Question #69

What is required in the fifth commandment?

Answer

The fifth commandment requireth the preserving the honour and performing the duties belonging to everyone in their several places and relations: as superiors, inferiors, or equals.

Eph 5:21; 1Pe 2:17; Rom 12:10

Question #70

What is forbidden in the fifth commandment?

Answer

The fifth commandment forbiddeth the neglect of, or doing any thing against, the honour and duty which belongeth to everyone in their several places and relations.

Mat 15:4-6; Eze 34:24; Rom 13:8

Question #71

What is the reason annexed to the fifth commandment?

Answer

The reason annexed to the fifth commandment is a promise of long life and prosperity (as far as it shall serve for God's glory and their own good) to all such as keep this commandment.

GOD'S GLORY

That your days may be long upon the land which the Lord your God gives you.

MY GOOD

Deu 5:16; Eph 6:2-3

Question #72

What is the sixth commandment?

Answer

The sixth commandment is, "Thou shalt not kill."

Exo 20:13

Question #73

What is required in the sixth commandment?

Answer

The sixth commandment requireth all lawful endeavours to preserve our own life and the life of others.

Eph 5:28-29; 1Ki 18:4

Question #74

What is forbidden in the sixth commandment?

Answer

The sixth commandment absolutely forbiddeth the taking away of our own life, or the life of our neighbour unjustly, or whatsoever tendeth thereunto.

Gen 4:10-11; 9:6 Matt 5:21-26

Question #75

Which is the seventh commandment?

Answer

The seventh commandment is, "Thou shalt not commit adultery."

Exo 20:14

Question #76

What is required in the seventh commandment?

Answer

The seventh commandment requireth the preservation of our own and our neighbors' chastity, in heart, speech, and behavior.

1Co 7:2-3, 5, 34, 36; Col 4:6; 1Pe 3:2

Question #77

What is forbidden in the seventh commandment?

Answer

The seventh commandment forbiddeth all unchaste thoughts, words, and actions.

Mat 15:19; 5:28; Eph 5:3-4

Question #78

Which is
the eighth
commandment?

Answer

The eighth commandment
is, "Thou shalt not steal."

VIII

Thou shalt
not steal.

Exo 20:15

Question #79

What is required in the eighth commandment?

Answer

The eighth commandment requireth the lawful procuring and furthering the wealth and outward estate of ourselves and others.

Gen 30:30; 1Ti 5:8; Lev 25:35; Deu 22:1-5; Exo 23:4-5; Gen 47:14, 20

Question #80

What is forbidden in the eighth commandment?

Answer

The eighth commandment forbiddeth whatsoever doth or may unjustly hinder our own or our neighbour's wealth or outward estate.

1Ti 5:8; Pro 28:19; Pro 21:17; 23:20-21; Eph 4:28

Question #81

Which
is the ninth
commandment?

Answer

The ninth commandment
is, "Thou shalt not bear
false witness against thy
neighbour."

Exo 20:16

Question #82

What is required in the ninth commandment?

Answer

The ninth commandment requireth the maintaining and promoting of truth between man and man, and of our own neighbour's good name, especially in witnessbearing.

Zec 8:16; Joh 5:12; Pro 14:5, 25

Question #83

What is forbidden in the ninth commandment?

Answer

The ninth commandment forbiddeth whatsoever is prejudicial to the truth, or injurious to our own or our neighbour's good name.

1Sa 17:28; Lev 19:16; Psa 15:2-3

Which is the tenth commandment?

The tenth commandment is, "Thou shalt not covet thy neighbour's house, thou shalt not covet thy neighbour's wife, nor his manservant, nor his maidservant, nor his ox, nor his ass, nor any thing that is thy neighbour's."

Exo 20:17

Question #85

What is required in the tenth commandment?

Answer

The tenth commandment requireth full contentment with our own condition, with a right and charitable frame of spirit toward our neighbour and all that is his.

Heb 13:5; 1Ti 6:6; Job 31:29; Rom 7:15; 1Ti 1:5; 1Co 8:4, 7

Question #86

What is forbidden in the tenth commandment?

Answer

The tenth commandment forbiddeth all discontentment with our own estate, envying or grieving at the good of our neighbour, and all inordinate motions and affections to anything that is his.

1Ki 21:4; Est 5:13; 1Co 10:10; Gal 5:26; Jam 3:14, 16; Rom 7:7-8; 13:9; Deu 5:21

Question #87

Is any man able perfectly to keep the commandments of God?

Answer

No mere man since the Fall is able in this life perfectly to keep the commandments of God, but doth daily break them in thought, word, or deed.

Ecc 7:20; 1Jo 1:8, 10; Gal 5:17; Gen 4:5; 7:21;
Rom 3:9-21; Jam 3:2-13

Question #88

Are all transgressions of the law equally heinous?

Answer

Some sins in themselves, and by reason of several aggravations, are more heinous in the sight of God than others.

Eze 8:6, 13, 15; 1Jo 5:16; Psa 78:17, 32, 56

Question #89

What doth every sin deserve?

Answer

Every sin deserveth God's wrath and curse, both in this life and that which is to come.

Eph 5:6; Gal 3:10; Lam 3:39; Mat 25:41; Rom 6:23

Section VIII

Faith & Repentance

What doth God require of us that we may escape His wrath and curse due to us for sin?

Answer

To escape the wrath and curse of God due to us for sin, God requireth of us faith in Jesus Christ, repentance unto life, with the diligent use of all the outward means whereby Christ communicateth to us the benefits of redemption.

Act 20:21; Pro 2:1-6; 8:33-36; Isa 55:2-3

What is faith
in Jesus Christ?

Answer

Faith in Jesus Christ is a
saving grace whereby we
receive and rest upon Him
alone for salvation, as He is
offered to us in the gospel.

Heb 10:39; Joh 1:12; Isa 26:3-4; Phi 3:9; Gal 2:16

Question #92

What is repentance unto life?

Answer

Repentance unto life is a saving grace whereby a sinner, out of a true sense of his sin and apprehension of the mercy of God in Christ, doth, with grief and hatred of his sin, turn from it unto God, with full purpose of and endeavour after new obedience.

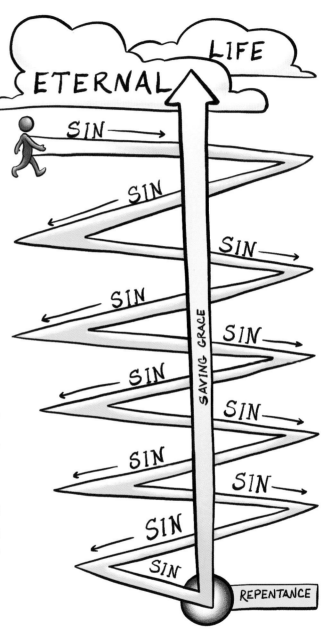

Act 11:28; Act 2:37-38; Joe 2:12; Jer 3:22;
Jer 31:18-19; Eze 36:31; 2Co 7:11; Isa 1:16-17

What are the outward means whereby Christ communicateth to us the benefits of redemption?

Answer

The outward and ordinary means whereby Christ communicateth to us the benefits of redemption are His ordinances, especially the Word, baptism, the Lord's Supper, and prayer; all which means are made effectual to the elect for salvation.

Mat 28:19-20; Act 2:42, 46-47

Question #94

How is the Word made effectual to salvation?

Answer

The Spirit of God maketh the reading, but especially the preaching of the Word, an effectual means of convincing and converting sinners, and of building them up in holiness and comfort through faith unto salvation.

Neh 8:8; Act 26:18; Psa 19:8; Act 20:32; Rom 1:15-16; 10:13-17; 15:4; 1Co 14:24-25; 2Ti 3:15-17

Question #95

How is the Word to be read and heard that it may become effectual to salvation?

Answer

That the Word may become effectual to salvation, we must attend thereunto with diligence, preparation, and prayer; receive it with faith and love, lay it up in our hearts, and practice it in our lives.

Pro 8:34; 1Pe 2:1-2; Psa 119:18; Heb 4:2; 2Th 2:10; Psa 119:18; Luk 8:15; Jam 1:25

Section IX
Baptism

Question #96

How do baptism and the Lord's Supper become effectual means of salvation?

Answer

Baptism and the Lord's Supper become effectual means of salvation, not for any virtue in them or in him that doth administer them, but only by the blessing of Christ and the working of the Spirit in those that by faith receive them.

1Pe 3:21; Mat 3:11; 1Co 3:6-7; 1Co 12:3; Mat 28:19

Question #97

What is baptism?

Answer

Baptism is an ordinance of the New Testament instituted by Jesus Christ, to be unto the party baptized a sign of his fellowship with Him in His death, burial, and resurrection; of his being engrafted into Him; of remission of sins; and of his giving up himself unto God through Jesus Christ, to live and walk in newness of life.

Rom 6:3-5; Col 2:12; Gal 3:27; Mar 1:4;
Act 2:38; 22:16; Rom 6:3-4

To whom is baptism to be administered?

Answer

Baptism is to be administered to all those who actually profess repentance towards God, faith in, and obedience to our Lord Jesus Christ, and to none other.

Act 2:38; Mat 3:6; Act 8:12, 36-38; 10:47-48

Question #99

Are the infants of such as are professing believers to be baptized?

Answer

The infants of such as are professing believers are not to be baptized, because there is neither command or example in the holy Scriptures, or certain consequence from them, to baptize such.

Exo 23:13; Pro 30:6; Luk 3:7-8

Question #100

How is baptism rightly administered?

Answer

Baptism is rightly administered by immersion, or dipping the whole body of the party in water, into the name of the Father, and of the Son, and of the Holy Spirit, according to Christ's institution and the practice of the apostles; and not by sprinkling or pouring of water, or dipping some part of the body, after the tradition of men.

Mat 3:16; Joh 3:23; 4:1-2; Mat 28:19-20;
Act 8:38; Rom 6:4; Col 2:12

Question #101

What is the duty of such who are rightly baptized?

Answer

It is the duty of such who are rightly baptized to give up themselves to some particular and orderly church of Jesus Christ, that they may walk in all the commandments and ordinances of the Lord blameless.

Act 2:41-42; 5:13-14; 9:26; 1Pe 2:5; Luk 1:6

Section X

The Lord's Supper

Question #102

What is the
Lord's Supper?

Answer

The Lord's Supper is an ordinance
of the New Testament, instituted
by Jesus Christ, wherein by giving and receiving bread and wine,
according to His appointment, His
death is shown forth and the
worthy receivers are—not after a
corporal and carnal manner, but
by faith—made partakers of His
body and blood, with all His
benefits, to their spiritual nourish-
ment and growth in grace.

Mat 26:26-28; 1Co 11:23-26; 10:16

Question #103

Who are the proper subjects of this ordinance?

Answer

They who have been baptized upon a personal profession of their faith in Jesus Christ, and repentance from dead works.

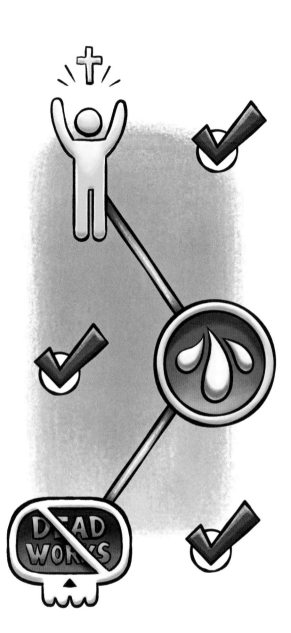

Act 2:41-42

Question #104

What is required to the worthy receiving of the Lord's Supper?

Answer

It is required of them that would worthily partake of the Lord's Supper, that they examine themselves of their knowledge to discern the Lord's body, of their faith to feed upon Him, of their repentance, love, and new obedience, lest coming unworthily they eat and drink judgment to themselves.

1Co 11:28-29; 2Co 13:5; 1Co 11:31; 1Co 10:16-17; 1Co 5:7-8; 1Co 11:28-29

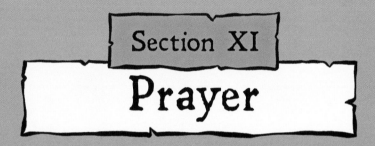

Section XI

Prayer

Question #105

What is prayer?

Answer

Prayer is an offering up our desires to God, by the assistance of the Holy Spirit, for things agreeable to His will, in the name of Christ, believing, with confession of our sins and thankful acknowledgments of His mercies.

Psa 62:8; Rom 8:26; 1Jo 5:14; Rom 8:27; Joh 16:23; Mat 21:22; Jam 1:6; Psa 32:5-6; Dan 9:4; Phi 4:6

Question #106

What rule hath God given for our direction in prayer?

Answer

The whole Word of God is of use to direct us in prayer; but the special rule of direction is that prayer which Christ taught His disciples, commonly called the Lord's Prayer.

1Jo 5:14; Mat 6:9-13; Luk 11:2-4

Question #107

What doth the preface of the Lord's Prayer teach us?

Answer

The preface of the Lord's Prayer, which is, "Our Father which art in heaven," teacheth us to draw near to God with all holy reverence and confidence, as children to a father, able and ready to help us; and that we should pray with and for others.

Mat 6:9; Rom 8:15; Luk 11:13;
Isa 24:8; Act 12:5; 1Ti 2:1-2

What do
we pray for in
the first petition?

Answer

In the first petition, which is, "Hallowed be thy name," we pray that God would enable us and others to glorify Him in all that whereby He maketh Himself known, and that He would dispose all things to His own glory.

Mat 6:9; Psa 67:2-3; Psa 83; Rom 11:36

Question #109

What do we pray for in the second petition?

Answer

In the second petition, which is, "Thy kingdom come," we pray that Satan's kingdom may be destroyed and that the kingdom of grace may be advanced, ourselves and others brought into it and kept in it, and that the kingdom of glory may be hastened.

Mat 6:10; Psa 68:1, 18; Rev 12:10-11; 2Th 3:1; Rom 10:1; Joh 17:19-20; Rev 22:10

What do we pray for in the third petition?

Answer

In the third petition, which is, "Thy will be done on earth, as it is in heaven," we pray that God, by His grace, would make us able and willing to know, obey, and submit to His will in all things, as the angels do in heaven.

Mat 6:10; Psa 67; 119:36; 2Sa 15:25;
Job 1:21; Psa 103:20-21

Question #111

What do we pray for in the fourth petition?

Answer

In the fourth petition, which is, "Give us this day our daily bread," we pray that of God's free gift we may receive a competent portion of the good things of this life, and enjoy His blessing with them.

Mat 6:11; Pro 30:8; Gen 28:20; 1Ti 4:4-5

132

Question #112

What do we pray for in the fifth petition?

Answer

In the fifth petition, which is, "And forgive us our debts, as we forgive our debtors," we pray that God, for Christ's sake, would freely pardon all our sins; which we are rather encouraged to ask because, of His grace, we are enabled from the heart to forgive others.

Mat 6:12; Psa 51:1-2, 7, 9; Dan 9:17-19; Luk 11:4; Mat 18:35

Question #113

What do we pray for in the sixth petition?

Answer

In the sixth petition, which is, "And lead us not into temptation, but deliver us from evil," we pray that God would either keep us from being tempted to sin, or support and deliver us when we are tempted.

Mat 6:13; Mat 26:31; 2Co 12:8

Question #114

What doth the conclusion of the Lord's Prayer teach?

Answer

The conclusion of the Lord's Prayer, which is, "For thine is the kingdom, and the power, and the glory, forever. Amen," teacheth us to take our encouragement in prayer from God only, and in our prayers to praise Him, ascribing kingdom, power, and glory to Him. And in testimony of our desire and assurance to be heard, we say, "Amen."

GLORY
HONOR
POWER

AMEN

THINE IS THE KINGDOM!

Mat 6:13; Dan 9:4, 7-9, 16-19; 1Ch 29:10-13; 1Co 4:16; Rev 11:20; 22:20-21

And Jesus came and spake unto them, saying, All power is given unto me in heaven and in earth.

Go ye therefore, and teach all nations, baptizing them in the name of the Father, and of the Son, and of the Holy Ghost:

Teaching them to observe all things whatsoever I have commanded you: and, lo, I am with you always, even unto the end of the world. Amen.

Matthew 28:18-20

Notes